Email Marketing:

The Ultimate Guide to Building a List Fast

Brendan Mace

Copyright © 2016 by Brendan Mace

Table of Contents

Introduction

Free Bonus

Chapter 1 – Getting Started

Chapter 2 – The Landing Page

Chapter 3 – The Instant Offer

Chapter 4 – The Email Series

Chapter 5 – Getting Traffic

Chapter 6 – The Results

Conclusion

Introduction

The money is in the list.

We've all heard that. You've probably even accepted it.

Have you ever questioned it?

Think about it this way. There are only two different types of traffic. There's traffic that you control and traffic that you don't.

Any free traffic from Google is uncontrollable. Sure, it's a nice bonus, and some of us will reap some excellent sales from it.

But you can't count on that.

The traffic from Google is controlled by… Well, you guessed it: Google.

A search engine may love your site today, but replace you with the next flavor come the next update.

And if history is any indication, Google updates are frequent.

Every time Google releases a new algorithm update there's a flood of decimated businesses banging on keyboards about their frustration.

You know what their mistake was? They relied on a traffic source they simply cannot control.

What we really need to focus on is the traffic that we control. If we can control our traffic, then we can have guaranteed results.

In order to control traffic, you need to pay for it.

A paid traffic source is not going to refuse to send you traffic. It's as simple as you paying for credits, and getting traffic in return.

My instinctual reaction to paid traffic is that free traffic is better.

After all, one option costs me money and the other one doesn't.

It turns out, my instincts were wrong.

Paid traffic is better because it is predictable.

You know, in many cases, exactly how much you're going to spend, and how many visitors you'll generate.

You'll also have a good idea at how much you can make from this traffic.

At that point, you really only need to focus on two numbers.

How much does each visitor cost you?

How much do you make from each visitor?

Are you getting it yet?

As long as you're making more than you spend, you can buy as much traffic as you want.

Instead of waiting for free organic traffic, you can buy thousands of eyeballs to your page in the next ten minutes.

That means, results are much faster and more predictable.

The tricky part is that you need to make more than you spend.

That's where list building comes in.

If you sent visitors directly to a sales page, you would probably make some sales. Not many, though, in all reality.

Why is that?

Because when you send a visitor directly to a sales page, it's usually their first exposure to your product.

This is what's known as cold traffic, and these visitors are stubborn buggers to convert into sales.

And it makes sense. How frequently do you buy a product you see for the first time?

For most of us, the answer is not that often.

Collecting an email address gives us an opportunity to promote more than once. It also lets us build a connection before slamming the sale.

Now instead of having a small chance of making just one sale, an email subscriber could buy dozens of products from our emails.

He remains as a potential customer on our list forever, or until he decides to unsubscribe from our list.

However, by that point, it's typical for an email subscriber to accrue far more revenue than a single cold visitor.

All we have to do is warm these subscribers up, and you'll be able to turn emails into cold hard cash.

This book will show you my blueprint for building a list and making easy money from it.

Enjoy!

Free Bonus

As a small token of thanks for getting this book, I'd like to give you a full course on how to make passive income online.

This training could easily be sold for $100's of dollars.

And in fact, people pay me significant amounts of money to show them how to make money online.

I'm willing to give you a slice of that freedom pie here.

Just visit this page, and learn my powerful Two Step Formula:

http://twostep.brendanmace.com

Part 1:

Part 2:

Part 3:

Find this Bonus Here: http://TwoStep.BrendanMace.com

This bonus is a 3-part video series that shows the process I've used to reach over $8,000/month.

In reality, my income since creating this video series continues to increase. I am happily expecting to make well over "Five Figures Per Month" on a consistent basis.

Whether you like reading or watching a video, I have you covered. My personal preference is to do both, and I recommend you use whatever learning style helps you the most.

I have an entire YouTube channel with 90+ videos on "making money online"

Over 19,000 people are subscribed to my channel, and many have figured this game out.

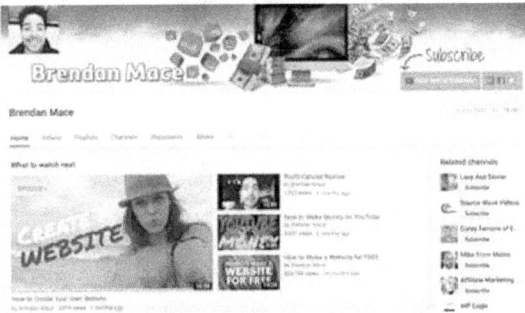

Join my YouTube tribe here: https://youtube.com/user/macbr9

Chapter 1 – Getting Started

I've been in this business for the better part of a decade.

Most of this email stuff I've learned from other email marketers, and a good portion I've developed from being in the trenches myself.

At this point, you may be asking yourself a bunch of questions. So let's answer some of them.

YES.

- I have done this stuff
- It does work
- It is legal

So let's get started…

The first step for any email marketer is to grow an email list.

Multi-millionaire email Marketer Ryan Deiss has this to say:

"One of the single biggest assets I have in my business is my email list. If you took away everything I had in business but left me with my email list, I could be back in business the very same day by making an offer to that list."

An email list is your ticket to online riches.

With a good-sized list, you can count on making money every, damn, day.

And best of all… It only takes about 10-20 minutes to set up emails.

Talk about a good income per hour.

There are a number of sneaky ways to build your following.

The most common method (and the one I recommend) I call:

Buy n' Build Free

The idea is simple. You only buy traffic with the fruits of your labor.

You may want to pump-in a little start-up cash. To get the thing going…

Once it's running, though, the whole system is fuelled by passive income profits.

Money in ==> -Instant Profit ==> Reinvest Money In ==> Instant Profit

And the cycle repeats, over and over and over…

This is the whole secret to email marketing

Creating a system (or funnel) that profits on ad spend

Sounds simple, right?

It is.

If you could make $2 for every $1 you spend, how much money would you invest?

A smart "marketer" would invest damn near everything.

And he'd double his money.

The key is to have a system that makes $2 for every dollar.

The following chapters will show you how to do it.

Chapter 2 – The Landing Page

Before anything else, you need a page that is designed to build a list.

When I started building landing pages a few years ago – I used to struggle A LOT.

Seriously – I'd spend hours (even days) creating my landing page.

The results were unsatisfactory.

I'd be lucky to get even a 25% opt-in rate. That's terrible.

Then a marketing friend gave me his landing page template.

What a nice guy.

Immediately my conversion jumped from 25% to 35%.

Still not the greatest, but I was making progress.

Now I have a 55.6% converting landing page. Tested on thousands of impressions.

Works like clockwork.

You can see it here:
http://twostep.brendanmace.com/

You know how long it took me to create this 55.6% lander?

The page was built in about 10 minutes.

No joke!

I use a done-for-you tool that creates 95% of the page for me. All you have to do is edit the text a little.

This tool is called WP ProfitBuilder.

It uses a template system to auto-create cool landers.

Templates sound boring.

In layman's terms…

WP ProfitBuilder is a done-for-you landing page creator.

That creates a page in minutes, like these:

HOT NEW ADDITIONS - Just To Make Things Even More Interesting...

Pretty cool, huh?

Instead of struggling to get a measly 25%, I can now get a 55.6% lander in the next few minutes.

And you can, too!

It works like this:

Take a template from WP Profit Builder.

Add in some text, and voila.

You have a guru-style squeeze page ready to rock.

Here's the one I adapted (in 10 mins) to get a 55.6% conversion rate:

To take a better look, this page is hosted right here.

Of course, there are other options on the market.

There's LeadPages, ClickFunnels, Landing Page Money, etc.

Tons and tons of landing page tools.

I haven't seen a single one that creates done-for-you pages in 10 minutes that are as affordable and high converting.

WP ProfitBuilder will damn near guarantee your success.

Chapter 3 – The Instant Offer

This is the whole secret sauce.

And probably where a number of readers will get offended.

Hey, this is the way email marketing works.

You need to spend money to make money.

We all know that's true, and so certainly in this case.

But where do we get the money?

With my blueprint, we get the money instantly.

Right after they sign up to our funnel.

Why?

If we can create a lander-instant offer combo that makes back what we spend on traffic, then we can easily achieve unlimited growth on autopilot.

Think about that one for a second…

If for every $1 we spend, we make $2. It's game over. We've won.

We do this by redirecting visitors to an instant offer.

A percentage of these visitors will buy. If enough new subscribers purchase the instant offer, then we will have self-replenishing traffic to our funnel.

So we need to pick an offer that converts into $$$

There are a few guidelines here:

1. The product should be in the $7-$27 range.
2. The product should have upsells galore.
3. The product should appeal to impulse.

Let's start with #1…

The product should be in the $7-$27 range.

I've heard it a million times before.

You should focus on selling high-ticket items. Your income will be much higher.

Even the outrageous claim:

The conversion rate for low and high ticket products is about the same.

Anybody that claims the latter is either selling you something, or has no idea what they are talking about.

The truth is, selling mid-high ticket items could be your best option on the back end of your funnel.

In other words, once people are <u>addicted to YOU</u>. They trust your advice.

Trying to sell a high-ticket product after opt-in is as about as likely as a homeless man selling you into his $997 mastermind group.

There's no trust yet.

Nobody is going to buy a $100+ product right after meeting you.

Or at least…. very, very few will.

So, your best bet is to pick a product that's cheap.

And yes, you won't make too much money on initial sales.

But here the tricky part…

The product has upsells.

So that means even if your initial sale only nets you $10. You could easily double or triple that profit on the upsells.

What's an upsell?

For the sake of clarity, an upsell is an offer that is presented after a customer makes an initial purchase.

So Joe blow buys your instant offer for $9.

You get $9 (or 75% of that)

Then Joe Blow is offered three upsells. Each one costs around $21. He buys TWO of them.

Now instead of making $9, you have made $51.

Sweet!

Brendan, show me an example!

No problem.

Here's one that I use called Copy. Paste. Hack.

This product sells at $9.

Take a look at the headline "Copy & Paste My $58,491 Per Month Campaigns & Start Using Them For Yourself…"

We want a product that appeals to impulse.

Any kind of "copy and paste" your way to success or make xxxx.xx amount per month.

These kinds of offers convert the best on impulse.

But wait, the best part…

Here's the offer's upsells:

After the initial purchase, there are <u>FOUR additional opportunities</u> to make a sale.

The instant offer sells at $9.95.

That's $10 per sale.

The upsells, though, are also high converting. And sell at even higher prices.

Even though your subscribers are only presented with a $10 offer. The average customer ends up spending around $20 per sale.

This $$$/sale is going to be really important later on. Keep it noted!

Now that we've picked an offer, how do we set it up?

Simple.

Go to your aweber account.

Or whatever auto responder you're using…

If you don't have one yet, pick up Aweber. It's 100% free for the first month. And other auto responder services have been known to give bad customer service and low delivery rates.

Once you're in, go to Sign Up Forms at the top header.

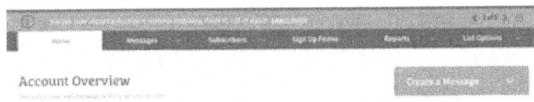

See it right between "Subscribers" and "Reports"

Cool!

Then click on "Create a Sign Up Form"

After saving your web form on the first page, the second page has the link settings.

This is where you set new subscribers to the instant offer.

It looks like this:

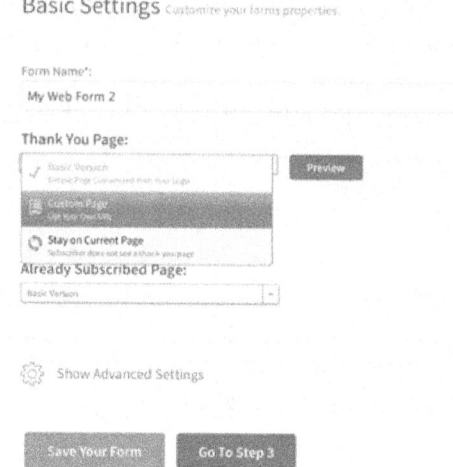

After clicking on "Custom Page"

Enter in your affiliate link, and you're ready to rock!

That's all for the initial set up!

Chapter 4 – The Email Series

Once set up, the first two steps can run on autopilot. I've had squeeze pages that have been set up for years. Take a look at this one – it's been around since 2011
The goal (up till this point) is to break even. Or maybe make or lose a bit.

With step #3, we want to make the REAL MONEY.

To get to "life changing income," we must focus on the back end.

Remember, subscribers will familiarize themselves with YOU. Which will make them a lot more likely to buy mid-high ticket products. That's where the life-changing profits are…

For this – we need an auto responder sequence.

A series of emails that will:

- Build a relationship
- Get traffic to your stuff
- Net you sales (make you $$$)

I have 154 emails in my sequence. It does ALL three of these things, and has taken years to build.

To ensure that you take action, and make it happen, I'm giving my entire sequence away for free.

Seriously!

You just need to copy + paste the campaign share code: awlist3794060-a1f00-$F

In your Aweber, hover over "Messages"

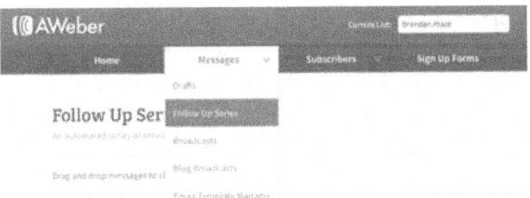

If you don't have an auto responder, then snag Aweber's 30-day FREE trial.

You'll be able to get my whole sequence. Which is easily worth $997.

This took me years to build, remember. I genuinely wish I had something like this offered to me when I started.

Go to a section about "Campaign Sharing"

It should look something like this:

Note: It may look different if you have no emails in your sequence.

It could also say something like "Looking for Campaign Sharing"

To which you say, "Hells yes!"

Enter the code

… And you'll instantly have my entire sequence. Holy smokes!

Chapter 5 – Getting Traffic

This section alone I could easily cram into a product and sell for $27, $37 or $57

Traffic is a big deal.

A lot of it is common sense. Some of it's a little ninja.

I'll be revealing everything.

The common sense traffic source
I've said this many times on my YouTube channel.

Solo ads are my favorite traffic source for email marketing.

They're:

- Easy
- Affordable
- Predictable

The best place to find them is on Facebook.

There are loads of groups that are dedicated to solo buyers and sellers.

Here's the one I created.

You can find at least a dozen more groups by Facebook searching "solo ads"

Some people get freaked out that they might get ripped off.
With a very brief rep check – this is unlikely.

Each solo ad seller lists his or her testimonials. And if they've been selling for longer than a couple months, they are not going to ruin their reputation over a single solo ad order.

I've purchased hundreds of solo ads, and I've been ripped off one time. I still ended up getting my money back…

So before purchasing any solo. Check for:

- Testimonials
- How long they've been selling

With just these two-step criteria, you can virtually eliminate all risk.

There are a few additional Q's to ask to improve ROI:

First of all, ask the seller "what are their list's interests?"

For example, I'll promote a list-building funnel. Sometimes when I ask sellers what their list is into, they honestly let me know that their list is more about Biz Ops or Niche Sites or MLM.

Each solo vendor has built their list with the exact strategies in this blog post. So, of course, their list is going to have certain preferences over others.

Another great question is about tier 1 percentage.

What the heck does tier 1% even mean?

I get this question asked a lot.

In this space, customers are constantly asking, "What tier 1% can you promise?"

And for good reason…

Tier 1 refers to the amount of subscribers that are from first world countries.

This sounds almost racist to request, but it makes sense, from a business standpoint.

Subscribers from third world countries, like India or Africa, are very unlikely to buy anything.

Which at the end of the day is your main goal.

This trend started a couple years ago in marketing. One day a Solo Vendor sold tier 1 leads for a more expensive price.

Suddenly, everybody wanted higher tier 1%.

In all reality, this is a positive marketing development. It does matter what country your subscribers are from. Their willingness to purchase is very much determined by it.

- A good tier 1% is 80%+
- An average tier 1% is 70%
- Anything under 70% is below average

Most times a solo seller is willing to guarantee a certain percentage.

Hold them to it.

What does a solo ad cost?

An average solo ad costs around .40-.45 per click.

That means if you buy 200 clicks, it'll run you $80-90

Some solo vendors charge more, others charge less.

For traffic, that's pretty darn cheap.

If you were to buy 200 visitors on Facebook PPC, or Google Adwords, it would almost definitely cost you more than 40 cents for each viewer.

When Your Business REALLY Takes Off!

Solo ads are great. They're cheap, affordable and predictable.

There's a traffic source that's even cheaper, equally easy, and more profitable.

… Trading clicks.

Once you have an email list, you'll be able to strike some trading deals with loads of marketers.

Same as with solo ads – the best place to find trading partners is on Facebook.

Here's that group again: https://www.facebook.com/groups/189347897917735/

To find even more partners to trade clicks with, Facebook search "ad swaps" or "click banking"

The power of click trading is immense.

Instead of having to pay $200 to get 500 visitors, now you can get 500+ visitors for no cost whatsoever.

Those 500 visitors all have a chance to buy your instant offer.

And, depending on your lander, half of them enter your backend. <– Sounds dirty

Remember – you have a funnel that makes more per visitor than 40 cents.

So for every partner you trade 500 clicks with, you can make much more than $200.

The Trading "Etiquette"

Trading clicks is mandatory. Insanely profitable.

There is etiquette to trading.

An unspoken rule that if you're the one contacting a banking partner, it's expected that you send the traffic first.

Don't worry, though.

If you pick partners that have a reputation, they will 100% return the exact number of clicks that you agreed upon.

My recommendation is to contact 20+ people, and ask to trade clicks with them.

The response rate is high with this outreach task, and usually over 50% will respond positively. Especially when you indicate that you're willing to send first.

If it's your first time trading clicks, and your list is smaller, it's wise to start with 100 click trading deals.

Side Note: Trading clicks is also known as "click banking"

In fact, the term "banking clicks" is becoming even more common.

These both mean the exact same thing. It used to be that ad swaps were traffic exchanges that happened on the same day. That's the way it worked. Now, one person sends first, and the other returns after they finish. That was the beginning of the "click banking" movement.

Must Have Traffic Tool

I get asked all the time, what are the tools that you NEED as a marketer?

clickmagick

This question hits at the root of success.

There are tons of products out there that have helped me get here.

Very few are CRUCIAL.

This one is: ClickMagick

What is ClickMagick? Why do I need it?

This is a link tracker – and it's the best in the biz.

A tracking link is critical to your success with list building.

It has a number of powerful benefits, like these:

- Notifies you of bot traffic
- Notifies you when links are down
- Tracks conversion rate
- Tracks quality of traffic (includes the tier %)

Bot traffic is becoming an increasingly challenging situation in MMO.

Fake traffic is not just useless – it's actually damaging to your list delivery.

Not going to get into all the geeky stuff here, but you should know that your delivery is impacted by how much your subscribers engage with your emails.

Fake traffic doesn't engage – that's a problem.

Your delivery will suffer.

ClickMagick automatically detects the legitimacy of traffic, and will instantly notify you by email when traffic is from robots.

Pretty damn cool!

And it's saved me from catastrophic headaches in at least a handful of transactions.

Advantage #2 is that ClickMagick notifies you when a link is down.

This happens every once and awhile, and can be fairly expensive.

Imagine buying a 500-click solo, and then realizing that your page was down the whole time.

Yep, that's happened to me.

There's no refund for a page being down. I had to eat the $200 loss and move on.

Having this feature for your tracker is big.

Of course, ClickMagick tracks your conversion rate.

This is crucial.

Free link trackers like bit.ly tell you how many clicks you've received. They don't tell you how many decided to opt-in to your email list.

That's the most important part.

You definitely want to know what sellers convert the best for your offer.

Sure, you could find a list online where people share which solo sellers gave THEM the best results.

The reality is that email lists are like snowflakes.

They're all different and respond differently to different offers <– That's a lot of difference.... You get the point!

With ClickMagick, you can easily see which seller's list converts for your offer.

Then you can DOUBLE your profit margin by reinvesting in sellers that convert.

And skipping the one's that don't make you a profit.

What about traffic quality?

Remember above when I said that tier 1% is taking this industry by storm.

ClickMagick is behind the movement 100%

A popular feature of this product is to set the outgoing tier%.

This is crucial when trading clicks.

Most partners will say, "let's trade 100 clicks at 70% tier 1%"

Without a tool like ClickMagick, you cannot control how much of your traffic comes from tier 1 countries.

That means that either:

1. You send too much tier 1% (hurts the ROI)
2. You send too little tier 1% (your trading partner is pissed)

It's too valuable to not buy. Get a good quality link tracker.

Chapter 6 – The Results

Clearly, this is the part we all want.

… And why not?

It's a pretty good gig, really.

It takes about 10-20 minutes per day to send an email.

I've seen guys make $40,000+/Month from their email list.

Pretty sick, right?

My email list makes me about $3,500/month

Some people may say:
"Wow, that sucks!"

To that… I say I have everything I need.

I have:

- No job
- No boss
- Freedom to live anywhere

Right now I'm in Medellin, Colombia with my beautiful girlfriend Caitlyn.

In the last 6 months, we've been to:

- The Okanagan
- Las Vegas
- Cuba
- Mexico
- Colombia

And we're planning a trip to the Dominican Republic this December.

With only 20 minutes per day for sending emails. We have the freedom to do what we want – when we want.

Having an email list feels like having a money faucet.

Whenever I want some money to hit a nightclub, or go pay my rent.

I just send an email to my list, and BOOM!
Money is made!

How to make money from the list

Your auto responder sequence + instant offer is your bread and butter.

Once set up, that will run on autopilot.

For extra money, you can promote through broadcasts.

There are three main ways I promote with my email list (plus a fourth bonus one)

1. Trading clicks
2. Selling clicks
3. Promoting clicks

The trading clicks are self-explanatory.

We covered this earlier in the post.

Find 20+ people that are trading clicks online. Ask them to trade with you!

The majority will say "yes."

Selling clicks is a little more maintenance – but not much.

You want to start building a reputation as much as possible.

That means asking for a testimonial from every person who receives your traffic.

It also may help to offer "testimonial copies" at the start.

Which means that you're willing to sell at a slight discount in exchange for the promise of a testimonial afterwards.

Of course, you'll take a small hit on your profit per transaction during this time. But you'll be setting yourself up to make more sales. And with a good reputation, you'll also be able to demand a higher price.

Testimonial pricing is a good long-term strategy for solo selling.

Selling solos is easy. Once you have your reputation, people will seek YOU out for business. There's no real hard selling involved. Just have a list that's capable of delivering good traffic.

The alternative to selling solo ads is promoting affiliate products.

I used to be mainly a solo seller, but I've now switched my business to focus on affiliate marketing.

It really depends on the value of your traffic.

When I send an affiliate promotion, my traffic EPC

(Estimated per click) is around .42 per click.

I used to sell solo ads for .35 per click.

But as I quickly noticed, my profit margin is higher through affiliate promotions.

Once you send out to your traffic, you'll be able to tell right away whether affiliate promotions or solo ads are more profitable. Whichever has a higher EPC is the one you should focus on.

Bonus Monetization Method – Covert Commissions

As an email marketer, I've tested dozens of list building products.

Most flop harder than a sumo wrestler attempting a back flip off a diving board. <– Good joke, right? Ha!

One of my favorite tools is Covert Commissions

This tool builds a list AND promotes for you!

Not only does Covert Commissions create a squeeze page for you. They'll actually send affiliate promotions on your behalf (with your affiliate link) for life.

Here are a couple examples:

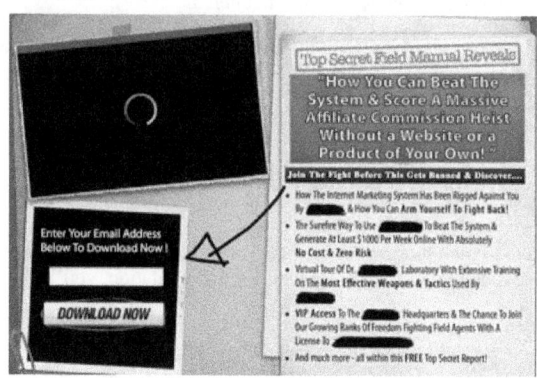

… And a second one:

Pretty cool!

Is Covert Commissions a Magic Bullet?

You know in Mario Cart Wii where you use a magic bullet to take your player from worst to first.

This is not one of those times.

I love Covert Commissions. But there's no such thing as a magic bullet in marketing or anywhere else in real life for that matter.

I promote Covert Commissions squeeze pages in my funnel.

And this does two things:

1. Gives away freebies to my list (makes me look cool)
2. Creates an additional autopilot income stream

The squeeze pages for this tool give away something of value.

Sometimes the freebie is a free report. In many cases, there's some really cool stuff. Like a list of 100 profitable niches...

Giving away these high quality freebies builds good will with your subscribers.

People are only going to buy from someone they know AND like.

These freebies give people a reason to like you.

PLUS...

It's an autopilot income stream that brings in a good income.

Because remember – Covert Commissions sends email promotions on your behalf, for life!

Over time, it's more profitable for me to send traffic to Covert Commissions than it is to send a standard affiliate promotion.

Sure, the day of an affiliate promotion, I will make a good chunk of change.

Over time, though, Covert Commissions will bring in WAY more sales.

It's a secret weapon that I use to increase my funnel ROI.

Here's a look at 8 of the 15 missions I use:

If you take nothing else from this post...

Knowing about Covert Commissions could change your business.

How much can you make with this stuff?

I get asked all the time, how much can you make per hour?

It really doesn't work that way.

The potential with list building is virtually unlimited.

This stuff also runs almost completely on autopilot.

I know email marketers that make $40,000+/month. I'm currently at the $3,500+/month and am continuing to grow.

The part that gets me is the 20 minutes per day.

The laptop lifestyle is my priority.

In marketing, people refer to these types of people as "digital nomads."

It means they can travel when they want to wherever they want.

Here's a thought provoking question for you...

If I told you that for every $1 you gave me, I'd give you $2 back.

How many dollars would you give me?

If you were smart, you'd give me near every dollar you have. Because you'd know that for every $1, you'd get $2 back.

The key is to build a funnel that makes more per visitor than you spend on traffic. If you can do that, you've won!!

What would you do with an autopilot $3,500+/month?

Imagine what you would do with this income stream.

Would you:

- Travel
- Support your family
- Go on vacation
- Quit your job

Everyone has a different reason for taking action.

What's yours? Figure it out, and make it happen!

That is – if you're up for what it means to be an email marketer.

That's the blueprint – what's your thoughts

This blog post could have easily been sold as a course.

It covers <u>damn near everything</u> to be successful with email marketing.

- Landing page
- Instant offer
- Auto responder sequence
- Traffic
- Making Money

Most of this stuff is above board. I know for sure, that some of my subscribers won't like the "instant offer."

However, that's how email marketers have the capital to reinvest into their list(s).

Is email marketing ethical?

My own personal opinion is that email marketing can be ethical and mutually beneficial. There are certain elements where your focus is to increase the ROI.

But, there's no reason why you can't add value along the way.

With:

- Blog posts
- Videos
- Tutorials

Any kind of freebie that helps your subscribers will do just fine.

List building should be a win-win for the marketer and the subscriber.

With great power comes great responsibility.

Now go out there and build your list!

Conclusion

This book shared how to build a list.

In order to make the most from this read, you need to take action on what you're learned.

If you have any marketing questions, you can always reach me at my main website: http://www.brendanmace.com

I am a full time entrepreneur and passionately enjoy connecting and helping emerging email marketers.

Do not hesitate to contact me!

If you find videos easier to follow than reading, I've created a 3-Part YouTube series right here on how I make passive income online. You'll see everything over my shoulder as I go through my main business model.

If you would like to learn more about email marketing, then I would love to chat with you. Check out my blog that shares in depth guides, like this one.

Right here: www.brendanmace.com

www.ingramcontent.com/pod-product-compliance
Lightning Source LLC
Chambersburg PA
CBHW070426190526
45169CB00003B/1437